NO LONGER PROPERTY OF
ANYTHINK LIBR
RANGEVIEW LIBRAR

D0842747

ALTERNATOR
BOOKS™

WHO INVENTED THE
TELEVISION?

SARNOFF VS. FARNSWORTH

Karen Latchana Kenney

Lerner Publications ◆ Minneapolis

Copyright © 2018 by Lerner Publishing Group, Inc.

All rights reserved. International copyright secured. No part of this book may be reproduced, stored in a retrieval system, or transmitted in any form or by any means—electronic, mechanical, photocopying, recording, or otherwise—without the prior written permission of Lerner Publishing Group, Inc., except for the inclusion of brief quotations in an acknowledged review.

Lerner Publications Company
A division of Lerner Publishing Group, Inc.
241 First Avenue North
Minneapolis, MN 55401 USA

For reading levels and more information, look up this title at www.lernerbooks.com.

Main body text set in Aptifer Slab Regular 11.5/18.
Typeface provided by Linotype AG.

Library of Congress Cataloging-in-Publication Data

Names: Kenney, Karen Latchana, author.
Title: Who invented the television? : Sarnoff vs. Farnsworth / Karen Latchana Kenney.
Description: Minneapolis : Lerner Publications, [2018] | Series: STEM Smackdown | Audience: Age 8–12. | Audience: Grade 4 to 6. | Includes bibliographical references and index.
Identifiers: LCCN 2017016646 (print) | LCCN 2017037107 (ebook) | ISBN 9781512483291 (eb pdf) | ISBN 9781512483192 (lb : alk. paper) | ISBN 9781541512115 (pb : alk. paper)
Subjects: LCSH: Television—History—Juvenile literature. | Farnsworth, Philo Taylor, 1906–1971—Juvenile literature. | Sarnoff, David, 1891–1971—Juvenile literature.
Classification: LCC TK6640 (ebook) | LCC TK6640 .K39 2018 (print) | DDC 621.3880092/2—dc23

LC record available at https://lccn.loc.gov/2017016646

Manufactured in the United States of America
1-43332-33152-8/18/2017

CONTENTS

INTRODUCTION
TWO TELEVISIONEERS

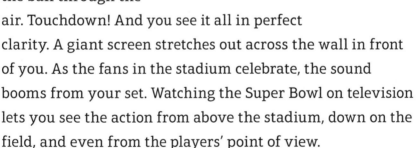

Time is ticking down on the biggest game of the season—the Super Bowl. Suddenly the quarterback finds an open man and launches the ball through the air. Touchdown! And you see it all in perfect clarity. A giant screen stretches out across the wall in front of you. As the fans in the stadium celebrate, the sound booms from your set. Watching the Super Bowl on television lets you see the action from above the stadium, down on the field, and even from the players' point of view.

Television has shared some historic moments with people around the world, from presidential debates to the first moon landing. But watching live events from your home was not always such a simple thing. Even a century ago, sending moving pictures with sound through the air seemed incredible, maybe even impossible.

This 1912 movie camera was called a kinetograph. Its movies were shown on the kinetoscope, a device that only one person could use at a time.

By the early twentieth century, the movie camera was recording moving pictures and radio was sending sounds through the air. Coming up with a way to merge these two technologies was the key to making television happen. In just forty years, television would become a phenomenon that swept across the United States.

But it was a difficult race to get to the first simple television **broadcast**. Two all-star competitors stood out from the rest. These two "televisioneers" would be on each other's heels to invent the first version of the television we know. The underdog was Philo T. Farnsworth, a farm boy turned scientist. The high-profile champion was the influential radio executive David Sarnoff. The battle would last more than a decade and cost millions of dollars.

CHAPTER 1

A TEEN GENIUS

Philo was eleven when his family moved to a farm near Rigby, Idaho. It was 1918, and his new home had something very exciting—electricity. Philo wanted to know *everything* about electricity. He started taking apart and building electronics and reading electrical and science magazines.

He read articles predicting a machine called television that would send pictures through the air. Several contenders had already stepped up to the plate to invent this new machine. Some were working on a mechanical kind of television, using moving machine parts to send and receive television broadcasts. But the results were slow and clunky, and the pictures never looked clear.

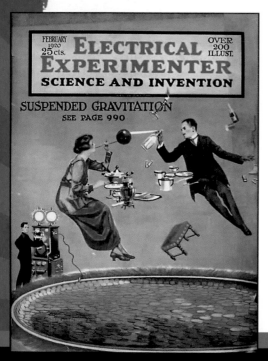

Philo learned all he could by reading science magazines.

ASSIST

German scientist Paul Gottlieb Nipkow (*right*) played a key role in inventing television. He created the Nipkow disk in 1884. It scanned an image through dots in a spinning metal disk. The disk was used in early mechanical television systems.

These systems ultimately weren't successful, but Nipkow's disks did pave the way for some early inventions in television technology.

In 1908, Scottish scientist A. A. Campbell Swinton suggested something different. He thought that television should be electronic, using **electrons** and electricity to scan and send images. Campbell Swinton believed it could be done by using a special tube and a stream of electrons. That tube just needed to be invented. That was what Philo, the young inventor, set out to do. At the age of thirteen, he started working on a game plan.

Incredibly, it wasn't long before he had an idea. In February 1922, Philo told his chemistry teacher, Justin Tolman, about his idea for a television tube. Philo even sketched it out. "The whole secret is controlling electrons," he told Tolman. Philo was just fifteen, but the young rookie had made his first big play.

HE DID WHAT?

In the summer of 1921, Farnsworth was plowing potato fields on his family's farm. The neat rows of potatoes gave him an idea for scanning an image. A picture could be scanned in rows and turned into electrons. Then the electrons could be arranged in rows on a television tube. He didn't know it yet, but this concept was key to making electronic television work.

Potato fields are planted in straight rows.

Farnsworth moved into his Green Street laboratory when he was just twenty years of age. He would make many of his breakthroughs in television in this lab.

ENTERING THE GAME

Farnsworth knew that to turn his idea into reality, he needed money to start a **laboratory**. So, at nineteen, he started assembling his team. He found **investors** and started experimenting.

By October 1926, he moved into a laboratory on Green Street in San Francisco, California. Farnsworth and his assistant Cliff Gardner worked on an image dissector glass camera tube. It would be able to scan an image and turn it into a stream of electrons. In early 1927, Farnsworth filed a **patent** for his camera tube.

Farnsworth finally transmitted a picture on September 7, 1927. The picture was only a black line, but the transmission definitely worked. Soon after, he filed another patent—this time, for an electronic television system.

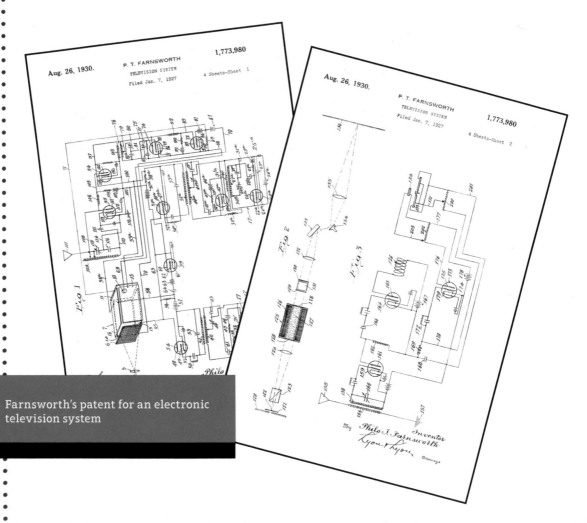

Farnsworth's patent for an electronic television system

Farnsworth demonstrated his invention, the first electronic television, to reporters who spread the word about the Genius of Green Street.

PLAYING TO THE PRESS

Farnsworth fine-tuned his machine, and about a year after his first successful transmission, he invited journalists to a demonstration on September 1, 1928. By the end of the month, headlines across the country reported Farnsworth's success. Finally, the world knew what was happening at the Green Street lab. Farnsworth was well on his way to victory. What Farnsworth didn't know was that another challenger—Russian-born American David Sarnoff—had his eyes on the prize too.

CHAPTER 2

THE RADIO EXECUTIVE

Sarnoff was a fierce foe with a savvy eye for business. He would prove to be stiff competition for Farnsworth, even though he wasn't an inventor himself. When he read about Farnsworth's advancements, he saw an opportunity to make money. His goal wasn't to make the television set himself but to own its patents. As the head of the powerful Radio Corporation of America (RCA), he knew the power of patents. Controlling them meant controlling an industry.

RCA held many radio patents. That meant it owned the rights of many radio parts. If

Sarnoff had the backing of a giant company behind him in his fight to own the patent for the television.

The Radio Corporation of America dominated the radio industry. This is a 1925 advertisement for an RCA radio.

other companies wanted to build and sell radios, they had to use RCA's parts and pay **royalties** for that use. Sarnoff saw the potential for the popularity of television. He knew that if RCA controlled the patents, it could make millions off televisions. But to do that, RCA would have to find its own pinch hitter. Farnsworth was in the lead, but Team Sarnoff was about to catch up.

Zworykin began working on televisions at Westinghouse Electric Corporation in 1919, but the company did not see value in Zworykin's work. He left Westinghouse to find someone new to fund his research. Here he is holding a cathode tube, which was a key part of his television set.

SARNOFF'S SCIENTIST

Sarnoff soon found his up-and-comer. Scientist Vladimir Zworykin was also working on an electronic television system and had filed patents for his invention. Zworykin met with Sarnoff in January 1929 to pitch his system. He imagined a **receiver** small enough to fit in a living room. Sarnoff decided to back his recruit.

As Farnsworth continued to improve his system, so did Zworykin. Although his camera tubes were not as advanced as Farnsworth's, Zworykin's television receiver produced a bright picture that was large enough for home use.

Zworykin demonstrates his television set. The invention broadcast images that were reflected onto a mirror that was angled above the screen. This allowed multiple people to watch it at once.

VISITING GREEN STREET

As Zworykin was picking up speed, Farnsworth faced a serious challenge. His investors were worried about his lack of progress in making a product they could sell. They wanted to make their money back, so they put pressure on Farnsworth to consider selling his patents and services to a bigger company like RCA.

Sarnoff was eager to make a deal. He was certain that with Farnsworth's patents, he would come out on top. He visited the Green Street lab in May 1931. Sarnoff offered to buy the lab, Farnsworth's patents, and his services for $100,000. Farnsworth flatly refused the insultingly low price, knowing the value of his patents.

Instead, Farnsworth teamed up with Philco, the largest seller of radios. Philco hired Farnsworth in June 1931 and agreed to pay royalties on his patents. Soon the company would begin making television sets using Farnsworth's tubes and receivers.

But Sarnoff wasn't going to let Philco and Farnsworth take the gold medal for television so easily. He had given Farnsworth a chance to join him. Now, with the power of RCA in his corner, Sarnoff would begin the real battle to own television.

Farnsworth continued making improvements on his television as he fought to bring it to the public. Here he is displaying his latest version of the television.

CHAPTER 3
THE PATENT WAR

In 1932, Sarnoff delivered the first blow. RCA filed a lawsuit against Farnsworth, claiming that his patent **infringed** on Zworykin's patent, filed four years before Farnsworth's.

Farnsworth (*center*) would be in a court battle over the infringement case for years. Here he is as he returned to court in 1939 to talk to a group of leaders in Congress about his difficulty in getting patents.

Farnsworth continued to work on his television during the court battle, even after he lost support from Philco.

Then RCA threw another punch, threatening Philco and sending a message to other radio manufacturers: Work with Farnsworth and RCA will not license its radio patents to you. Soon after, Farnsworth and Philco separated. Without the backing of a major company, Farnsworth was a free agent again.

HE DID WHAT?

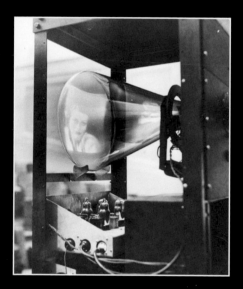

Farnsworth broadcasted an act with actress Joan Crawford during his demonstration. In this photo, Crawford's image is being projected on the television cathode tube.

In 1934, Farnsworth held a public demonstration of his electronic television at the Franklin Institute in Philadelphia. He put a camera by the door of the exhibit, and visitors saw themselves on the receiver. Farnsworth also set up different acts to broadcast on another television every fifteen minutes. He put on politicians, musical acts, and even trained monkeys! People lined up for blocks to see this new wonder.

TOLMAN'S TESTIMONY

Meanwhile, the patent lawsuit dragged on in the courts. Farnsworth claimed he first had the idea in 1922, but how could he prove it? Then he remembered his chemistry teacher. Amazingly, Tolman still had the drawing Farnsworth had given him. The teacher testified, and Farnsworth's side was boosted. But what hurt RCA the most was that Zworykin's system ended up being very different from his original patent. On July 22, 1935, the ruling came in. Farnsworth was the inventor of electronic television.

Even after RCA attempted to **appeal** the decision, Farnsworth was the victor. The inventing powerhouse had won the battle. He was able to move forward with his plans to start a small television company with a few close friends in the summer of 1937.

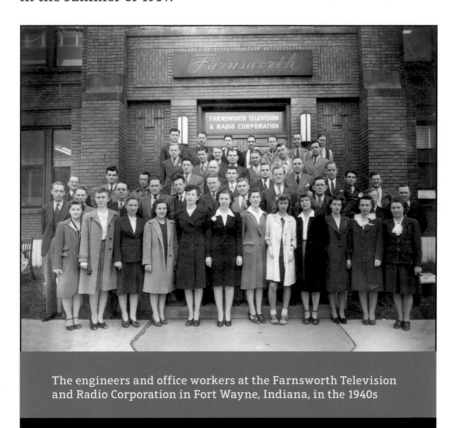

The engineers and office workers at the Farnsworth Television and Radio Corporation in Fort Wayne, Indiana, in the 1940s

CHAPTER 4

THE FATHER OF TELEVISION?

Undeterred by the lost court battle, Sarnoff and RCA plowed ahead and perfected their televisions. However, they had to use some of Farnsworth's parts. That meant that if they ever wanted to sell their sets, they'd have to pay Farnsworth.

On April 20, 1939, RCA held a publicity event to launch their televisions. In front of a television camera at the RCA building, Sarnoff stepped up to a podium. He declared, "Now we add radio sight to sound." Newspapers wrote about RCA's launch of this new industry, but Farnsworth's name wasn't

The RCA Victor TRK 12 (*above*) was one of the United States' first consumer television sets.

Sarnoff's speech on April 20, 1939, marked the first commercial television service broadcast.

even mentioned. Although he had been legally declared the champion, Farnsworth was falling behind.

While Sarnoff was leading RCA into the new era of television, Farnsworth struggled. He didn't have RCA's resources or money. It wasn't an equal race, and Sarnoff was pulling ahead. Yet Sarnoff still wasn't able to completely knock out the champ. He knew he'd have to pay Farnsworth royalties. This would be a first for RCA. In September 1939, RCA and Farnsworth came to an agreement. RCA would pay Farnsworth's company $1 million over ten years plus royalties.

THE BODY BLOW

Although he had finally reached an agreement with RCA, Farnsworth faced an even bigger competitor—the public market. In 1941, the United States entered World War II (1939–1945). All factories had to start making supplies for the war. Nobody was making televisions. A few years after the war ended, Farnsworth's key patents expired, meaning that

Farnsworth knew that the global conflict that would become World War II could take years off the useful life of his patents. Still, he worked hard to make his television as successful as possible.

During World War II, factories in the United States focused their efforts on making supplies for the war. They did not have time to produce televisions.

anybody could use the technology without paying him a cent. Just months later, television sales took off, but Farnsworth was left behind.

RCA promoted Sarnoff and Zworykin as the inventors of television in a TV special that aired in January 1949. RCA was the leading maker of televisions, while Farnsworth was forced to sell his company later that year. The Radio-Television Manufacturers Association would later give Sarnoff the title Father of Television.

The television has brought the world together to witness history in the making, such as the first moon landing.

A disappointed Farnsworth faded into the background as RCA took over television. He had invented TV, but RCA received all the credit. Still, Farnsworth's imaginative invention made a great impact on the world as we know it. When Farnsworth watched the historic 1969 moon landing broadcast on his own television set, he knew it could never have been shown without the technology he had invented. He told his wife, "This has made it all worthwhile."

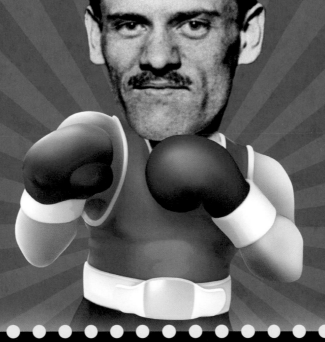

THE WINNER!

FARNSWORTH

INVENTOR MATCHUP

SARNOFF

- **POSITION:** Business executive
- **GOAL:** Fortune
- **AGE WHEN ENTERED INTO THE TELEVISION BATTLE:** 38
- **BACKING OF A BIG BUSINESS OR SOLO:** Big business

VS.

FARNSWORTH

- **POSITION:** Inventor
- **GOAL:** Learning through inventing
- **AGE WHEN ENTERED INTO THE TELEVISION BATTLE:** 15
- **BACKING OF A BIG BUSINESS OR SOLO:** Solo

TIMELINE

FEBRUARY 1922
At the age of fifteen, Philo Farnsworth sketches a tube he wants to make for an electronic television system.

1923
Zworykin files patents for his version of an electronic television.

1927
Farnsworth files a patent for his television system.

SEPTEMBER 1, 1928
Journalists visit Farnsworth's lab, and news of his television spreads around the world.

JANUARY 1929
Sarnoff hires Zworykin to develop an electronic television system for RCA.

1932
RCA sues Farnsworth for infringing on its television patent. Farnsworth eventually wins.

SEPTEMBER 1939
RCA agrees to pay Farnsworth a $1 million fee plus royalties for use of his television parts in their sets.

1947
Farnsworth's key patents expire, so he is no longer able to collect royalties on televisions. Soon after, television catches on as many people buy sets for their homes.

SOURCE NOTES

8 Daniel Stashower, *The Boy Genius and the Mogul* (New York: Broadway Books, 2002), 25.

22 Ibid., 237.

26 Ibid., 258.

GLOSSARY

appeal: to ask for a court's decision to be changed

broadcast: a program sent out for television or radio

electrons: tiny particles that move around the nucleus of an atom and carry a negative electrical charge

infringed: to have violated the rights or laws of another person or company

investors: people who give or lend money to an inventor or company with the understanding that they will get a share of any profits

laboratory: a place that contains special equipment for people to use in scientific experiments. *Lab* is short for *laboratory.*

patent: a legal document that gives an inventor the right to be the only person to make or sell an item

receiver: a piece of equipment that receives radio or television signals and changes them into sounds or pictures

royalties: sums of money paid to the owner of a patent for use of the patent

FURTHER INFORMATION

Hamby, Rachel. *Televisions*. Mendota Heights, MN: North Star Editions, 2017.

Hamen, Susan E. *Who Invented the Light Bulb? Edison vs. Swan*. Minneapolis: Lerner Publications, 2018.

Marsico, Katie. *Tremendous Technology Inventions*. Minneapolis: Lerner Publications, 2014.

NBC Universal: Our History
http://www.nbcuniversal.com/our-history

Otfinoski, Steven. *Television: From Concept to Consumer*. New York: Children's Press, 2015.

Philo T. Farnsworth's Invention
http://historytogo.utah.gov/utah_chapters/from_war_to
_war/philotfarnsworthsinvention.html

The Story of Philo Farnsworth: The Kid Who Invented TV
http://www.kidzworld.com/article/19948-the-story-of-philo
-farnsworth-the-kid-who-invented-tv

The Story of Television
https://archive.org/details/0578_Story_of_Television
_The_13_37_07_00

INDEX

PHOTO ACKNOWLEDGMENTS

The images in this book are used with the permission of: iStock.com/Irena Tsoneva, p. 1; iStock.com/Dmytro Aksonov, p. 4 (football player); iStock.com/fad1986, p. 4 (television screen); Hulton Archive/Getty Images, pp. 5, 12; The Advertising Archives/Alamy Stock Photo, p. 6; ullstein bild/Getty Images, p. 7; ESOlex/Shutterstock.com, p. 8; Matthew Kiernan/Alamy Stock Photo, p. 9; U.S. Patent #1773980, p. 10; Bettmann/Getty Images, pp. 11, 14, 17, 20, 23, 27 (Farnsworth), 28 (Farnsworth); SuperStock/Alamy Stock Photo, p. 13; Acc. 90-105 - Science Service, Records, 1920s–1970s, Smithsonian Institution Archives/Wikimedia Commons (public domain), p. 15; Everett Collection Historical/Alamy Stock Photo, p. 18; Special Collections, J. Willard Marriott Library, University of Utah, pp. 19, 21, 24; Jacklee/Wikimedia Commons (CC BY-SA 4.0), p. 22; Universal History Archive/Universal Images Group/Getty Images, p. 25; NASA, p. 26; iStock.com/lushik, p. 28 (boxing gloves); Archive Photos/Stringer/Getty Images, p. 28 (Sarnoff). Design elements: iStock.com/ivanastar; iStock.com/Allevinatis; iStock.com/subtropica.

Front cover: Archive Photos/Stringer/Getty Images (Sarnoff); Bettmann/Getty Images (Farnsworth); iStock.com/Irena Tsoneva (television); iStock.com/Allevinatis (boxer).